ZIG ZAG ZEN

ZIG ZAG ZEN

A ZENTERESTING COLORING BOOK

VALERIE CARR

NORTH LIGHT BOOKS
CINCINNATI, OHIO
www.artistsnetwork.com

INTRODUCTION

You know that feeling you get when you realize that some things are just meant to be? That's what came to mind when the opportunity arose for me to create this book.

More and more, research has shown the multiple benefits that adult coloring books provide—especially when it comes to relieving stress. Just like meditation, coloring gives us a chance to escape the everyday hustle and bustle, de-clutter our thoughts and plug into the creativity within ourselves.

As a meditator of twenty-plus years, I am delighted to be able to combine my drawing skills with a project that is connected so closely to mindfulness. As you zig-zag your way through the fanciful, quirky pages that follow, it is my hope you will awaken your creative spirit and find your Zen.

ABOUT THE AUTHOR

Valerie Carr is an artist, illustrator and maker. She is the pen, paper, needle and thread behind Valerie Valerie, translating her artwork onto products such as greeting cards, stationery, coloring books, fabrics, wallpaper and wall art.

Working from her bright and tidy garden studio in Shenfield, England, she paints and illustrates in watercolor and ink. Her style is a contemporary take on the traditional with a mix of quirky line drawings of architecture and animals, watercolor florals and vibrant repeating patterns. Valerie also loves to experiment with hand and machine embroidery, creating embroidered pictures using her own fabrics.

Visit her at **valerievalerie.co.uk** and **facebook/VVgreetings** to learn more.

DEDICATION

This book is dedicated to Dylan Carr-Purcell for teaching me how to roar exactly like a lion while I was illustrating *Zig Zag Zen*.

 Other fine North Light Books are available from your favorite bookstore, art supply store or online supplier. Visit our website at fwmedia.com.

21 20 19 18 17   5 4 3 2 1

DISTRIBUTED IN CANADA BY FRASER DIRECT
100 Armstrong Avenue
Georgetown, ON, Canada L7G 5S4
Tel: (905) 877-4411

DISTRIBUTED IN THE U.K. AND EUROPE
BY F&W MEDIA INTERNATIONAL LTD
Pynes Hill Court, Pynes Hill,
Rydon Lane, Exeter, Ex2 5AZ
United Kingdom
Tel: (+44)1392-797-680
Email: enquiries@fwmedia.com

ISBN 13: 978-1-4403-4936-2

Edited by Christina Richards
Designed by Anita Cook
Cover designed by Geoff Raker
Production coordinated by Jennifer Bass

Ideas. Instruction. Inspiration.

Receive FREE downloadable bonus materials when you sign up for our free newsletter at **artistsnetwork.com/ Newsletter_Thanks**.

Find the latest issues of *Cloth Paper Scissors* on newsstands, or visit **artistsnetwork.com**.

These and other fine North Light products are available at your favorite art & craft retailer, bookstore or online supplier. Visit our websites at **artistsnetwork.com** and **artistsnetwork.tv**.

 Follow North Light Books for the latest news, free wallpapers, free demos and chances to win FREE BOOKS!

Get your art in print!

Visit **artistsnetwork.com/splashwatercolor** for up-to-date information on *Splash* and other North Light competitions.